To Josh:
I appreciate
our friendship, you
have always been
straight with me. Within
this book is a small depiction
of my life in the land we
call America. I & have you
been pleasant but you
always learn with the help of God
to adapt to any situation
Enjoy
Bill Ferrell
[signature]
7/2015

A Letter to the Right

A Letter to the Right

by

William Ferrell III

Senior Publisher
Steven Lawrence Hill Sr.

Awarded Publishing House
ASA Publishing Company

BBB ACCREDITED BUSINESS

A Publisher Trademark Title page

ASA Publishing Company
Nominated for the 2012 Better Business Bureau Torch Award
105 E. Front St., Suite 101, Monroe, Michigan 48161
www.asapublishingcompany.com

Book: A Letter to the Right
Date Published: 07.16.2013
Edition: 1 *Trade Paperback*
Book ASAPCID: 2380623
ISBN: 978-1-886528-63-5
Library of Congress Cataloging-in-Publication Data

This book was published in the United States of America.
State of Michigan

A Letter to the Right

Table of Contents

LETTER OF SUPPORT

For Joan Denise Ferrell, Sharon & Samuel Snorton, Ivy Miller, William Ferrell IV, Kyna Ferrell, Delana Evans, Art Mobley, James & April Forbes, Mae Williamson, Thomas Benge Jr, Altheria Newman, Brenda Smith, Kenneth Gilbert, Fred Chapman, Eileen Chapman, Joe Martin, Dorothy Ferrell, Greg Smith, Robert Gates, Valerie Chapman, Cleveland and Martha Barnes, Annice Snodgrass, Gwendolyn Fort, The Elzy Family, The Sharber Family, Irvin Hayes, Cindy Jeffers, Etta Wilson, Larry and Linda Walker, Pastor D. Norflette Mersier, Jr, Pastor Anthony C. Campbell, Pastor Jack E. Ealy, Pastor William Ferrell Sr, Pastor William Ferrell Jr, Pastor Joe Jordan, Frances Isabelle Ferrell, Andrew Coleman, Lorraine Dexter, Marguerite Bodiford, Dr. Raymond Campbell, Tessie Conte, Gwen Matthews, Gus Dixon, Janice Estmond, Linda Patton, Eddie Payne, St. Paul CPCA, Bondine Rushton, and Pastor Julius C. Hope.

I love you all and thanks for your support in all that I do…..WF3

(b)

Preface

This book is dedicated to African American's who work in Corporate America, to the Managers, Supervisors, Administrators in a leadership position be it by your hard work or the Branch Rickey's in your life that opened a closed door for you to walk through. To the stares that you have had to endure, to the indifference you've experienced the second class citizen syndrome that you have been exposed to. To those of you who have faced racism openly or indirectly this is for you also. For the moments that you felt you were not worthy I am saying to you emphatically that you are. We are a strong people, a loving people, a family oriented people who have been led astray by whitewashed racism in sheep's clothing, and you know who they are. To my loving wife of blessed memory Joan Denise Ferrell who helped me endure the rigors of pastoring, to Dorothy Ray Ferrell who witnessed my struggle with Corporate America and what I had to go through without really knowing the depth of my experiences. To Gwendolyn Fort and her total support at a time when I needed it, I say thank you. To my sister who I can always count on Sharon Oretha Snorton and all of my kids, Bud, Ivy and Kyna I only did what I did to inspire you to higher heights by showing you the attributes and rewards of hard work. To friends and acquaintances that have encouraged me to use the gifts that God has given me to reach the masses. I love you all more than words can say.

Introduction

I have been black all of my life, not only have I been black all of my life......God saw fit to bless me with enough melanin in my body where there would be no doubt at all about my ethnic orientation. That is not the case always with some of my black brother's and sister's (more on that later). I now am in my twilight years almost 69 soon and I have outlived both my father and grandfather and I am grateful to God for that. My father passed at the age of 61, but since he was born February 12, 1894 and was 50 years old when I was born after 19 years of marriage to my mother, the medical field has come a long way. Not only have I been black all of my life I have also been an American all of my life, even though I'm labeled African American now, that in itself is amazing seeing how I actually started out being colored, oh well! I have watched this country which I love (I'm also a veteran and served three years in the Army and was honorably discharged 1963 – 1966) turn into right and left, conservative and liberal, socialist and activist etc., these catch phrases have drove me crazy. I have listened to those on the right spew there animosity towards my President, those of color and those who are less fortunate by no choice of their own, who have been caught up in a system that works against their equal citizenship, retribution, job opportunities, decent housing in locations other than the so called ghetto etc. Those conveyors of this vehemence are Rush Limbaugh, Glenn Beck, Mark Levine, Bill O'Reilly, Shawn Hannity and others who make up the Fox News Network and others.

Through the Fox Network and conservative radio stations located throughout America. They have screeners on their shows so that most folk can't get a word in; if they do they are cut off in the middle of their statements and then vilified by the host. So these guys have it good they only talk to folk that agree with their views and there are a lot of folk that do, trust me. The founding fathers (former slave owners) since President George Washington have basically run this country and I dare they blame all of America's faults on a black President that has only been in office for four plus years, how stupid is that. Whenever I here this type of excuse it makes me wonder about my Caucasian brothers for sure and whether they need mental help or actually believe that hogwash, unfortunately I think it is the latter that they espouse to. The reason for this book was because of the awakening that I had through reading. My mentor of blessed memory Dr. Anthony Cordova Campbell's philosophy was read everything and remember fifty percent. Reading is knowledge and knowledge is power I only wish that my people would do more reading. Unfortunately I am going to have to use the "N" word basically because it is in the title of the book that I read that inspired this writing. I hope that after you read this book you will know about the Force that we live under here in America, from the founding fathers (former slave-owners) to the present day.

"**The Force**" (Excerpt from N. Quamere Cincere's book – "We Ain't No Niggas! Exposing the Deception of Your World History Education." There is an intangible force that currently perpetuates the concept of white superiority and black inferiority. This force also plays a role in the assumption that a black man in a big expensive car is a drug dealer and a white man in the exact same car is a go-getter, a young professional advancing his way up the corporate ladder. The Force in the form of your history classes has an overarching power that affects all subjected to it. Many are touched by the Force without ever realizing it. If you have ever done any of the following acts, then you have fell victim to the power of the Force.

1. If you have ever referred to any person of color as a nigga, nigger, or however you want to spell it (even if you are black).
2. If you have ever used the phrase 'niggas and flies, the things I despise' (again even if you are black).
3. If you have ever used the term 'forget that nigga' or forget 'em, they're just niggas.'
4. If in a professional setting, you have ever thought to yourself 'what are they doing in here' whenever a person of African descent walks into the meeting room.
5. If you have ever made the assumption that a person of color with expensive material possessions was a drug dealer.

6. If you have ever been shocked to see a person of African Descent in any professional position of power (like our President).
7. If you have ever fought for racial segregation.
8. If you have ever felt the impulse to move out of a neighborhood just because blacks moved in.
9. If you have ever clinched your pocketbook just because you came into proximity to a young black male.
10. Any black that ever moved out of the way of a white person or let a white get in front of them simply because that person was white.
11. Any white that expected to get in front of a black simply because they were black.
12. If you ever showed a general lack of respect towards a person of color simply because they were a person of color, then you have been affected by the Force.[1]

Expression of any of these scenarios demonstrates how the force has directly affected you. After reading this my

---

[1] N. Quamere Cincere, *We Ain't No Niggas Exposing the Deception of Your World History* (California, Maryland: *Know*ledge of Self Publishing, LLC, 2007). 13

whole life of sixty-eight years came clearly into perspective, thusly I had to write this book for those folk on the right with prayerful consideration as my guide.

A Letter to the Right

by William Ferrell III

Chapter 1

How I Started Out

I guess by normal standards I was blessed to have a father and a mother to raise me, not that it is necessary because my mother after my father's demise would also become a single parent so I can relate to both of those scenarios. The only difference with my story was that in the fifties there wasn't a terminology (latch key children) that described my mother's position the only identifier that I had was when I left for school in the morning she was there and when I got home in the evening she was there also with dinner prepared. Please don't accuse me of that barefooted and pregnant mindset nor the idea that a women's place is in the home, the women I have been associated within my life have all been opinionated and independent in their thinking and I accepted it. But in hindsight I feel blessed that my mother was always there and that I wasn't home alone or in a day care center or a relative's house, there is nothing like a mom at home. I was spoiled to a degree, oh yes my parents knew how to tell me no and they would do it quite often, that is why I eventually worked for myself especially after my father (a prominent pastor in the city of Detroit) passed. I had my customers both white and black, that was a little before white flight or the suburbs. I maintained their lawns be it by raking leaves in the fall (I would pride myself in getting every leaf up to have nothing but green showing when I finished my job that work ethic would later bless me in life to reach heights I could have never imagined) I also shoveled snow in the winter. I packed groceries, had a paper route and remember to this day the overwhelming joy that I felt when I enabled myself through practice and lot of papers in the bushes to have my papers rolled in my paper bag and being able to throw them onto the perspective porches while steadily moving on my bike, "boy was I bad or what." My mother couldn't afford some of the clothes that I wanted to wear, that was before gym shoes, my generation wore Ben B. Burks, Stetson's, Stacy Adams, Alpaca Sweaters, Gabardine Hi-Lo Shirts, Silk Shirts, Ban-Lons and Leather Jackets with our shirt collars out over the collar, we were coordinated from our underwear to our socks, pants, t-shirts and shirts. I went to Central High School in Detroit and a lot of my classmates were from well to do families, doctors, lawyers and professional people that is because we lived near Edison, Chicago Boulevard, Boston Boulevard, Longfellow, and LaSalle Boulevard all streets that by those present day standards housed the cream of the black community. So my school was labeled an "Elite" school meaning mostly high yellow blacks as they were called to almost white in complexion. We had two clubs that I can remember the Hexagon's and Minor Quo Ques I was the darkest thing to associate with them. You see the Force was present then our minds were all convoluted by color even within our own race, inadvertently trying to be white. Not literally but hypothetically realizing that if anything it meant a better station in life, their houses were bigger, their schools wiser, their refrigerators fuller, their cars nicer I could go on and on and it still continues today the only thing is they are now willing it seems to do anything to keep the status quo in tack relative to wealth in America. Let me also reiterate why I was spoiled you see my father as I write this book was born on the same date as Abraham Lincoln just a different year, he was born February 12, 1894 yes I know this is 2013 am I crazy! Let me explain, my father was a Pastor and for nineteen of the thirty years that they were married my father pastored in Kent, Ohio, in Cincinnati Ohio (the New Prospect Baptist Church) he was also the first pastor of Dexter Avenue Baptist Church (1925) in Detroit, Michigan eventually returning to Detroit in 1940 as the first pastor of the New Grace Baptist Church now located in Highland Park, Michigan (back then it was on 92 E. Forest and John R. So for nineteen years my mother was barren, so as she put it when it seemed that something was moving in her stomach she thought it was a tumor or something because at the time she was 38 and my father was 50. So she went to see Dr. Guy O. Saulsberry a prominent physician of extraordinary dedication, great compassion for his people and administrative capabilities (eventually building the Kirwood Hospital in Detroit, Michigan) in a time when no black was reaching that type of plateau in our city, my, my, my what a role model for a fellow to aspire to. When my mother visited Doctor Saulsberry he informed her that she didn't have a tumor, she was pregnant so for eleven years I was not only a preacher's kid but a spoiled one, I never will forget when I joined the Boy Scouts my father spent about $1,000.00 just on Boy Scout stuff I still have a knife and a few other items to this day. I would be remiss not to mention Dr. Robert Bennett also a prominent black physician, who for a time was Joe Louis' doctor, he too was a good friend of my family, these were the examples that I had, these are the examples that the black community needs to keep reproducing over and over again, but the Force has kept this from happening. We aspire to being drug dealers, hustlers, gamblers and common thieves to reach financial security and the powers that be the controllers of the Force create laws and build prison's to house us when we ere. I was astounded to read that the law banning the use of cocaine was created directly because of us. There was this fear that the white man had of his women being exposed to a Mandingo type black man high on cocaine to ravish their women. The Force has kept that active to this day when one can obviously see the relationship of the punishment handed down for crack cocaine (more prevalent in the black community) more than powdered cocaine (more prevalent in affluent communities) all one need do is to get in their car and just drive through various areas in conjunction to their neighborhoods and you will see where affluence lives. This scenario is sort of ironic about cocaine when you realize that at one time it was mixed into Coca-Cola. My own son even fell victim to the punishment rendered by those on the so called right Reagan and Bush when they put into effect these Maximum/Minimum jail punishments rendered to those who were caught up in the cocaine hustle and because of this my son had to spend 10 years of his life in Federal Prison (from 22 – 32) with no chance of parole for good behavior or anything. He was just a part of the billion dollar a year prison system lining the pockets of my white brothers at the expense of others, the Force indeed is alive and well. I was a smart little fellow in Elementary School in a time when kids who showed this type of attribute, were double promoted. I don't believe that is even done anymore. What this meant was I would always get my work done first and then mess with the other kids as they worked to get their work done and I always received stars or A's for my effort, which really wasn't an effort at all. So I was double promoted from the 2B to 3B and later double promoted from the 4B to 5B, they wanted to do it a third time and my mother said no. So when I got to Junior High School I discovered girls, became the class clown (I could have been a comedian in another life, I'm sure) so I flunked a year, but still managed to get out of school a year ahead of myself. When I got to High School under the able mentorship of Ms. Ollie McFarland the former head of the Music Department for the schools in the City of Detroit, I again say what a line-up of positive role models to aspire to. Our school was the first to present a full-fledged opera Carmen by Bizet (I was El-Remandado) we later performed Aida. So I sang my way through High School, also being a part of an annual function given once a year when the most gifted of music students would gather at Wayne State University both white and black. They would pass out sheet music to us and with no rehearsal at all, just the knowledge of being able to read music we would be given our pitch and then proceed to sing the whole song with its varying parts in a glorious symphony of sound, what a time, what a time. I even sang at my graduation with Preston Willingham, James Crockett of blessed memory and Gary Burns. We also performed as a

Barbershop Quartet, later adding Bronson James who replaced Gary Burns. We even sang for the then Mayor of Detroit, Michigan, Jerome Cavanaugh. The able Mrs. Volker was the architect of this group along with the Troubadours', we could surely sing. I would be out of school and go back in the afternoon to attend a couple of music classes that I received no credit for, I just loved music that much (still do). I had a scholarship offered to me by Wayne State University (I wanted to go to Juilliard in New York) but because my mother raised us on ADC (Aid for Dependent Children) she couldn't afford the $2,000.00 needed to start me out I remember her feeling so bad about it. I told her to fear not that I was going to the Army, I eventually arrived in Europe and would later audition for the Seventh Army Soldier's Chorus (I made it) and also the R&B group that I sang in the Vel's, won the all Nurnberg Post Contest in 1964 I still have the silver plate from that event. I am a licensed Barber, Nail-Technician and received two Master Degree's while in my 50s, I always did my wife's (Joan Denise) hair and nails and all of the cooking she was spoiled and I did it. She passed on June 26, 2011. I eulogized her on the 1st of July. I am also working on a book about the 7 ½ years that I took care of her after a major stroke in September of 2003 its title will be "Love In Sickness and in Health" please look for it. I also have pastored two churches and served as the second Alumni President to my Alma-Mater Ashland Theological Seminary Detroit Center the main University is located in Ashland, Ohio. These are the abilities and circumstances that I bring to the table, not too shabby I must say but because I have always been somewhat of a non-conformist I am often ostracized either by gossip or jealousy (I must say two of the biggest enemies of the black church to this day). Just based upon this outsider's mindset that follows me, I can write this book no holds barred because I've lived long enough to be able to tell the truth and let the chips fall where they may. I also pray continually for those who are under the umbrella of Christian reconciliation but don't practice it. We must learn as the Bible teaches that if you have umbrage with a brother or sister go to them, talk it over. Black folk we need to talk more with one another, my wife always did that with me and through those conversations we had a definite understanding and respect for one another. I've often said that two of the hardest words for us to say as individuals is "I'm Sorry."

Chapter 2

My Stories While Living Under the Force

Is there an age when one can first realize the influence of the Force? I don't believe so because while each individual has their own story or recollection it comes at different times in each person's life. My first recollection of the Force wasn't a negative experience like the others I will cover, but it was unique in and of itself. There are recollections of your childhood that hold so many secrets that you can't always emphatically relate to, so you need the help of someone else of worth to help you relate to the circumstances of said event. With me it was this particular event that my mother (Frances Isabelle Elzy Ferrell) helped me to identify. I was good and grown when I went to her with this question. I asked her one day, "mother" it seems I remember a couple of white people that came to our home once a year, they would stay at our house because I remember the lady holding me on her lap etc., and something else I remember it seems that the man drove this white van and on the side of the van he had painted some scriptures on it and there was a black hand shaking a white hand, was I dreaming this. My mother looked at me and smiled and informed me that I wasn't too far off in my recollection. She said that a few years back my father ran a revival for a preacher who lived in West Virginia on one of his visits down there he met this preacher I believe his last name was Jones. There spirits connected so much so (mind you this was in the 50s) that your father invited Reverend Jones to come up to Detroit and run a week long revival for him. When they came to Detroit they insisted on staying at our home rather than a hotel and thus the relationship started. I thanked her for clarifying the incident for me, you see I do believe that prejudice is taught to you starting at a very young age or it's not taught to you, you then form a sense of tolerance for your fellow man regardless to their color. Point in fact one day when I was living in Mt. Clemens Michigan many years ago my ex-wife (Dorothy Ray Ferrell) used to work at the St. Joseph Hospital on Crocker Boulevard. It was a summer day and normally I would have driven to pick her up from work but on this day I said that I would walk the five or six blocks that it would take me to get there and then walk back home on such a beautiful summer day together. As I approached this one particular block, I noticed this little white boy and black boy playing together they were having a great time. As I drew closer unbeknownst to the little white boy his grandfather with grey hair who had come to the front door beckoned him to come in the house. Just before I was directly in the front of the house the old man says, "What did I tell you about playing with that nigger boy?" I will never forget the look on the grandfather's face when he all of sudden realized that I was walking by in hearing distance; he scurried back into his house with a quickness. But here some thirty-five years later this is indelibly etched in my mind. These are the things that I carry and that many black folk carry that seem to indicate that we are different realizing all along that there is nothing different in us at all. I remember in Seminary a professor of mine Dr. Zimmerman noted to us once in class that he didn't know what all the fuss was about, all you had to do is look at us and realize that we are all human beings not from monkeys as are attributed to black folk sometimes in a negative way. But created by a Supreme Being the I Am God in his own image. White folk have two eyes, black folk have two. White folk have two hands, black folk do too. White folk have two legs, black folk do too. Unlike the story that a nurse told me who frequented my home in service to my wife after her stroke, that in her particular circle it was actually thought that black folk had a longer bone in their legs to cause them to run faster, I was astonished. No our running is not from an over extended bone length, it comes from years of running from white folk trying to do us harm. I call that self-preservation don't you guys on the right agree? This leads me to another myth about my race that I was astounded to learn about in my youth. I joined the service in 1963 and spent three years in the Army until 1966. Being stationed in Furth, Germany in the prime of my youth 18 – 21 I did things that any other red blooded young man would do, pursued many Fraulein's. In fact I almost married a Fraulein named Gisela and have often wondered over the years how different my life would have been if I would have married her, one thing for sure she was "sehr schön" (very beautiful) and I loved her dearly. Before I connected with Gisela there was this particular night that I picked up a young Fraulein at a Guesthouse that I frequented, I believe her name was Renaada (this was a long time ago). After we left the Guesthouse we went to a motel and during the process of you know getting ready to you know, I noticed that she kept trying to look behind me to the point that it was getting very obvious that something wasn't right. So I said to her very abruptly "vas ist los" (what's wrong). She asked me where my tail was! "I said my tail," what do you mean, she said her former boyfriend who was of the Caucasian persuasion who frequented the Guesthouse that you know played their kind of music you know how we conjugate with one another (that's one of our problems also). I love country music and guess what I really love Bluegrass for some reason, I don't know why. Music has been called the language of the God's it touches all of us in a special way regardless of ethnicity. She said he also told her don't ever mess with a black guy their genitals are twelve inches long and they will tear you up. "I don't know about that I guess I must be white when it comes to that charge and I have seen some white boys that ought to be ashamed of themselves," Nuff said. But the Force always adds an indifferent explanation when it is applied to us. After I assured her I didn't have a tail and wouldn't rip her apart with the baggage I was carrying we proceeded to have a lovely evening with one another (I must say the first of many). So let me go another step further to show you how prejudice is taught and passed on from generation to generation if it is allowed to perpetuate itself. One day as I was working at the Tank Arsenal located in Warren, Michigan the gentleman who had hired me (Howard Burns of blessed memory, wife Willa of blessed memory also) was talking to me and I can't remember how we got on the subject of Germany the war etc., but we did. All of a sudden Howard who had served in World War II said yeah and I hope they don't come at us with that story about us having tails. I said whoa, wait a minute Howard you mean to say to me that lie was being used in the 40s? He said oh yes, I thought my, my, my they are passing this lie on from generation to generation, could they have done that with our history also I ask? My mother used to say to me, "Son something in the milk ain't clean." You figure it out. These lies also have been due to the Force that has been relegated to us over the years. I carry this around also as to my supposed inferiority, which I don't claim in one iota as being who and what I represent, hogwash fellows on the right pure hogwash, take your lies elsewhere. I have plenty of sense educationally speaking and common sense also, they used to call it years ago in my community "mother wit." There are a lot of black folks that realize that no matter what you say with a straight face or crooked face it is all pure hogwash, it makes me wonder who the real buffoons really are? Back in the 50s my father had his left leg amputated up to his left knee due to diabetes. We took him to the University of Michigan Hospital in Ann Arbor, Michigan they had a remarkable track record at the time for being a major health institution. I never will forget this one day that my mother my two aunts, my cousin and sister and my uncle had gone to visit my father. It was a little distance from Detroit and it afforded us some time to enjoy each other's company like black families use to do. So finally on the way home the suggestion came up to stop at a hamburger place and get some food to eat in the car on the ride back to Detroit. All were in one accord to the suggestion, so myself along with my uncle went into this hamburger place, mind you it wasn't in my mind to look for signs saying "no blacks allowed" or black's go to the back entrance" I was a young boy hungry for a cheeseburger, fries and milkshake. I can't remember what my uncle told the white waitress and as I think back all the occupants in the restaurant were white, there must have been the stares (I'll address that later) but I was totally removed from such things. So he ordered all cheeseburgers, accept a plain burger for my cousin who always ate his burgers and hot dogs plain, uhhhh! He ordered French Fries a few milkshakes and pops, so with such a big order naturally it took awhile to get everything passed out. When that was finally done as we opened our cheese-burgers (supposedly) which we had paid the full price for according to the menu posted in the restaurant we noticed that all of us had cheese sandwiches with all the condiments, ketchup, mustard, relish and so on, but one primary ingredient was missing the meat! My aunt Bill (they didn't call her Bill because she was overly feminine, they called her Bill because she was a tomboy, played baseball with the guys and could whip the average man with her fist.) wanted to go back to the restaurant and "kick the waitresses, you know what." We were able to calm her down and hesitantly ate our expensive cheese sandwiches and fries on the way back to Detroit. This remembrance I attribute to the Force also and I have remembered that experience over the years also, wondering if I was different or inferior for some reason, hogwash I say pure hogwash Rush. When you get a group of white boys together you have a problem one on one it was different and normally nothing would occur that was egregious. Standing on the corner once off of LaSalle Boulevard in Detroit before "white flight" when white folk still stayed in some of our (African American) neighborhoods. A car load of them passed me by almost running up on the curb calling me "nigger" as they laughed moving on at a high rate of speed. Or the night I was going home to Mt. Clemens, Michigan where I lived at the time from a night of partying in Detroit. As I was driving down Gratiot Avenue once again a carload of my white brothers drove by at a high rate of speed moving into my lane a few hundred feet in front of me and someone started throwing cork bricks out of the window that would bounce backwards and eventually bang against my grill. When I couldn't take it anymore I proceeded to speed up passing there car on the right hand side and in one moment hit my glove compartment as if I was reaching for a gun and came up real fast with just my index finger pointing to the occupants of the car, literally scaring them to death, there was a median that ran down the center of Gratiot that had a very high curb to it, the driver immediately made a sharp left turn over the median with the occupants hitting their heads on the roof of the car in the process trying to get out of my way, I laughed all the way home. But yet an still, it was the Force that subjected me to this treatment anyway, why is it wrong for anyone to drive their car home regardless to the time of day or night, all they really want to do is get home, but many have been killed with just a simple trip like that in mind, sad so very sad. As I continue let me say, oh yeah the stares this is something that I don't understand about my white brother's and sister's when I have entered certain establishments over the years, it is as though they stop everything that they are doing and go to staring at me. No it's not my imagination it is very real and I'm quite sure if you ask your black friends they would let you know that, I have asked my white friends (because some of my best friends are white) about it. My polish friend of blessed memory Bob, who I worked with me at Goodyear, told me this and I've never forgotten it. He said "Bill I feel sorry for your race because some of the stereotypical actions directed towards you are based in part upon your exclusivity." I said elucidate Bob if you will, well with the white race you have the Polish, the Italians, the French, and WASP etc. With you they pool their opinions into one bag when they look at you all they see is a black person, an African and regardless to your worth you are pooled into that one big grouping of blackness. I thanked him for that and have never forgotten it, listen white folk I may get by on $1,600.00 a month in my old deprived age, but guess what I love escargot, beluga caviar, Bentley's, fine wine when I could drink it, foie gras, oysters, filet mignon, beef cheeks, lobster, lump crab, Peking duck, pirogue's, mortadella, stuffed cabbage, beef goulash, prosciutto, Cristal champagne, a good schnitzel, frog legs, quail, collard greens and chitterlings also, wait a minute can a black person be an Epicurus, you bet they can even if you keep all the money and fine things to yourselves. We know about them let me continue, I used to work as a Store Manager at Goodyear Tire and Rubber Corporation, I will address that more in my chapter on Affirmative Action. But anyway I was a Store Manager for Goodyear and a friend of mine, another store manager Caucasian in persuasion was selling a car, we came to an agreement and made the deal all I had to do was to drive to his house in Warren, Michigan to pick it up. So one day after I had closed my store, my wife had come with me to work on that day because she wanted to see the car first hand (keep those ladies happy) so she spent the day at my store looking at TV and visiting with the employees and making sure that I took her to a fine lunch with all the trimmings. So we proceeded to my friend's house there were no cell phones then as I recollect. My wife was a Nurses Aide and after she had dressed to go to work I said to her do you want to go to the store with me today you know I am picking up our car, which is when she said she wanted to go with me never really changing out of her Nurses Aide whites. So here we go up to the house that I had the address, now mind you my wife is dressed like a nurse and I am in my corporate getup you know shirt and tie and big brogan wing tipped shoes that all the executives wore back then, I wore mind with pride because they were a reminder of who I felt I was and also who I was capable of being, more on that later. It was a nice summer day no need for coats or the like, so I proceeded to ring the doorbell, I rang it again and again, then I proceeded to knock on the glass which is the natural progression that all of us take, still no response. All of a sudden I look up and a Warren Police car is pulling up in front of the house, they proceeded to get out of the squad car hands over the tops of their holsters as they approached me and my wife. Their first question was 'why was I there' not hello, we got a call from someone at this address saying you were here, no just very bluntly and coarse, "What are you doing here?" I proceeded to tell them that I had purchased a car from another Store Manager that I worked with and he asked me to come by his house to pick the car up on that day and I had also brought my wife with me because she wanted to see it also. I cautiously reached in my pocket and gave him one of my business cards that stipulated I was in fact a Store Manager for Goodyear, my wife then showed them her I.D. as a Nurses Aide for the St. Joseph Hospital in Mt. Clemens. The officer lightened up just a little bit, not a lot but said that at the moment the only occupant of the house was the mother of my friend and she was scared to open the door because I looked like the guy that had robbed their store a few months back (I immediately thought of what Bob had told me about that grouping we were placed in, we are all black and evidently we all look alike, the Force at work). By then I'm getting a little testy and said do I look like a robber, my wife is in a nursing uniform, I'm in a shirt and tie doesn't that count for anything it's obvious I'm not carrying a weapon. The officer apologized (finally) and said that it would probably be better if we would leave and wait until we could connect with the gentleman that I was buying the car from with certainty before I came back. The next day I received a call from Chuck, he was so embarrassed (I could tell) that he knocked $500.00 off the purchase price to make amends, naturally I accepted his generous offer and assured him that I had no umbrage towards him or his mother and I also asked him to apologize to her for (I wanted to say for being black) my causing her some discomfort, the Force at work. Once again you carry these things in your everyday life when you approach a store, when you see folk coming towards you as you pass them by in a public parking lot. That leads me to another story of the Force and how it works. I worked with a guy at the Tank Arsenal whose name evades me at the moment as we talked one day about nothing in particular but eventually we got on the subject of race and how some of the white folk acted at the arsenal. I worked with folk that would talk to me at work and if I saw them in a supermarket in the close proximity of my work place where I had probably stopped to get something on the way home. I would see the individual maybe as we approached each other in the same isle I would speak (the guy's name was Walter) looking directly at this person and he wouldn't say a word. It would make me so angry that I would say as he passed, "well Walter your damn ears must be full of wax not to speak with your ignorant butt," and proceed on with whatever I was going to get, oh yeah I was much bigger than Walter and probably could have waxed him very quickly if I needed too. But then you lower yourself to his level. I'm so glad to have a President whose civility and intelligence is a plus to me for this time, I am so proud of him and his accomplishments. I had already remarked to a few friends that I love to controvert with on different subjects) that if George Bush got eight years that ought to be the new tenure for all President's henceforth.

When I tell my friends that at one time there were three African Pope's they are astonished with that information but research afforded me the opportunity to look at these men and most of them look white they were just born or lived in Africa when elected the maps of the world were quite different then and folk that were Roman were born and lived in Africa. So then the question is were they really black? I say also that the last one was elected approximately 1,500 years ago and you can rest assured that there are those that don't want another black president for that same length of time and he is even half Caucasian. But be encouraged he did get re-elected for a second term because to me his intelligence, civility and rationale out shined that other guy of dubious credibility. Back to my story, so my co-worker said to me that one of the hardest things that he had to adjust to when he moved up North was to not step in the street when he saw a white person approaching him, I was floored. Now mind you I'm a Northern Boy and if you don't move out of my way my shoulder might cause you to stumble, I had never thought of nor experienced that particular subjection due to the Force. I said to him "are you serious?' he informed me that he was indeed serious after being raised in an environment that he was forced to do that. How can one not feel inferior being subjected to that hogwash, God bless those of blessed memory that had to endure that unwarranted subjection of indifference and inferiority, due to the Force. I thought of my time as a young man of eighteen years of age, fresh in the Army and stationed at Ft. Jackson in South Carolina now mind you my mother being of an over protective nature, didn't want me to join the Army, when I drove a cab in Detroit she didn't want me to do that, if I had an altercation her first reaction would be to call the police, that was my mother. She was born in Indianapolis, Indiana moving to Ohio and then Detroit and only heard and read about things that happened in the South and we all know about those things Emmet Till, Medgar Evers, Martin Luther King, Jr. I could go on and on. So she had already told me emphatically don't leave the base don't go into town, I promised her that I wouldn't (right). So on the second week of A.I.T. I took a pass and went into town this is in 1963. When I got into the downtown area it wasn't very big but had the normal businesses located therein. I was on one side of the street and I noticed a sign in a Barber Shop window saying "No Blacks Allowed" now being a Northern boy I had never seen nor heard of such things. Then I noticed an old black man inside of the Barber Shop shining the shoes of a patron, that blew me away the circumstance of a sign on the front window saying no blacks allowed and a black man doing work inside of the Barber Shop, duh! Who's the buffoon here, the black man or the Barber Shop owner you figure it out? As I looked across the street I noticed a bunch of black kids standing in line at what appeared to be a movie theatre (some of the girls was really cute, thereby qualifying them for the smooth attack of Private Ferrell hailing from the "Big D." I got into the back of the line but as I got closer to the window where you pick up your ticket I noticed what was really going on. A young person would go up to the window and say I want to buy a ticket to the movie, the ticket salesperson would then say no, she would be asked why by the young person, the ticket person would say because you're black, then that young person would come behind me and stand in the line again. All of a sudden I noticed this big fat white guy (sort of like well I won't call his name you know who I'm thinking about) standing over to the left of the ticket window chomping on a big cigar hanging out of his mouth and a great big 45 stuck inside his belt against his fat stomach for everyone to see, I said to myself whoa...........if my mother knew where I was and the situation I was in she would have, well I won't say. So I felt compelled to go through this process and get to the window also, doing the same thing that I had seen the other young black teenagers doing, only when it was my turn to go to the back of the line I approached the fat white guy standing to the left of the window I just said to him

"You know you ought to be ashamed of yourself standing up here with that big cigar in your mouth and that 45 tucked in your pants for everyone to see, you just ought to be ashamed." His mouth was hanging wide open with the cigar barely holding on to his lip before falling out of his mouth, I'm sure he probably never had a black person to talk to him that way, but I did I had it like that. Rather than go to the back of the line I crossed the street just before a Paddy Wagon drove up (this was so surreal) and started loading all of the young people into it with them singing the anthem of the Civil Rights movement very loudly "We Shall Overcome." My mouth was hanging open and as sure as God gives me breath right after the Paddy Wagon had pulled off (I will never forget this) I noticed a white man walking down that side of the street holding hands with a black woman that seemed to be his girlfriend. I immediately hailed a cab and told him to take me to the black community and cement streets, turned into asphalt and then into dirt (I was in the black community!) I had arrived, little did I know that there were two HBCU colleges there Benedict and Allen and on that weekend Grambling was coming to town and I knew about the marching band, it turned into a great weekend. I eventually met a lady old enough to be my mother that took me into her home, she would talk to my mother and give me keys to her home just based upon the fact that I was a good boy and for six of the eight weeks I was there I would go into town let myself in and stay at her house, one weekend she wasn't even there she had to go out of town but she trusted me and I respected her trust with reciprocal trust (good old southern hospitality for sure). She is probably gone now but I want to thank her for being a representative of how our community used to be, built on trust and not distrust her name evades me now. I remember talking with my mother one evening and she informed me that when they lived in Kent, Ohio black folk would stop by their house periodically at varying times of the day and night and ask was this the home of Pastor Ferrell. When my mother said yes they asked if they could stay there for the evening and my mother said she would always oblige them. I said "mother" folk would stop at your house that you didn't know, eat dinner with you and then you would pack them some food to go on their way normally to some convention or religious meeting somewhere, she said yes. I said wow! She said son you must remember this was a time that we couldn't stay in hotels and motels so we had to have our own travel network (The Green Book of Negro Travel). The Force even controlled where we could or couldn't stay. Thanks again to God's grace and mercy that provided for our ancestors in a way that we need to learn and talk about again, folk nowadays would stay in your house and steal you blind, strip the copper and everything else if you let them in. There are still decent people in the black community, because I know a lot of them myself. A few more stories about the Force and its influence. Over this past Thanksgiving Holiday after a fine meal with family as we sat around talking, we got on the subject of race; you see black folk talk a lot about racism amongst their peers. That is because the Force has caused us all to be leery about white folk and even Congress lately. You see this gentleman had bluish green eyes, hair like a white man and was very light (like they say in my community almost white). He told us stories about him staying in the better hotels, eating at the finer restaurants, going to nice clubs etc., because of his complexion. He told us that if the white folk that he was around even had an idea that he was black, he would have been lynched or hurt very badly for sure. He also told us that after hiring in with one of the big three in Detroit he eventually made foreman because the powers that be thought he was white. He remembered a company party that they had when he finally decided to give his co-workers a hint as to who he was so he took his wife (who was black) the final consensus was that he was involved in an interracial marriage. He told us about a time when a battery exploded into his face and a co-worker also of African descent. He called his wife and she rushed to the hospital and as soon as she got there they took her to the black man, she informed them "this is not my husband that is my husband over there" their mouths fell open. Another high school buddy told me how his father of Mexican descent told him to say he was white because of his fair complexion and straight hair, so he could get a job and he did. The things he heard white folk say about black folk caused him even to have a few altercations, he couldn't believe what he was hearing. I then added a story of mine when I was a Store Manager for the Goodyear Tire & Rubber Company (more on that later) one of my customers was named Joe and his last name sounded like it was Italian I can't remember it exactly, but Joe was a pleasure to talk too he had a little swagger about him but he also had straight black hair was light complected and talked with what seemed to be an accent. One day he brought his car into the store to be serviced, he came into my office and informed me that his wife would be in later to pick the car up. My office was near the cash register, I heard a lady come up to the counter and give Joe's last name, but my mouth fell open this lady was black as shoe polish (no lie). I came to my door and introduced myself and told her to tell Joe thanks for the business, she told me that she would. Trust me I couldn't wait to see Joe again and finally one day he came into the store I immediately grabbed him and took him into my office, I said "Joe I didn't know that you were married to a black woman, he replied Bill I'm black" I was speechless. He then proceeded to tell me the same stories that I had heard over the Thanksgiving Holiday. He informed me of all the times in his younger days how he frequented fine night clubs dated white women and everything. He also talked about being in certain situations that if there was even an assumption that he was black he knew that he would have been killed. You see within the black race we come in all shades white folk cannot produce anything but white off-spring. According to an article in 2009 Amon Hotep entitled ("Black Skin Is the Genetic Parent") he states in part.[1] "Always remember these points and you should never have to hold your head down to any recessive genetic defects. All phenotypes exist within the black family. Asian people are only the semi-recessive descendants of their ancestors who were a black African tribe with slanted eyes. White people are the albinos of a specific group of Africans and have inherited those people's phenotypes. They try to imply that their phenotypes were originally theirs and that if you see people of African descent with these features, they inherited them from white people.

[1] Article written by Amon Hotep entitled "Black Skin Is the Genetic Parent" 2009.

Nothing is further from the truth. Blacks are the genetic parents. Remember, whites cannot reproduce anything else but themselves. They cannot reproduce genetic material they don't have...melanin. Therefore, they cannot reproduce us, but we can reproduce them and all others in humanity." These last two stories explaining the power of the Force for this particular chapter. I was in the town of my Seminary, Ashland, Ohio and on one occasion my wife (Joan) and I stopped by a restaurant to get sandwich. As I got out of my van walking into the restaurant I noticed these two elderly Caucasian women sitting by the window. They both were staring at me and my wife with such unfeigned sincerity that I stopped in my tracks and just stood there staring at them, so much so that my wife told me "don't do that Buddy, I said why not they are doing it to me what's wrong with us, we're dressed nicely and not indigent" yet again these stares are a direct influence of the Force that exist in America it goes on and on and is alive and well, don't fool yourself believe it! Finally my sister Sharon told me about her encounter with the Force while working for a department store a seemingly wealthy Caucasian lady brought her items to the cash register to pay for them, as my sister processed her purchase she had some change to give to the lady. As she reached to give the lady the change, she quickly moved her hand causing the change to fall everywhere. Then she said to my sister "I did that because I didn't want you to touch my hand" now my sister in her youth could not be deemed a peacemaker she could fight like Layla Ali. She punched some Caucasian lady in the mouth at the supermarket after she made a comment saying "I hate seeing those afro's that black people wear", my sister popped her in the mouth causing the lady to fall back and knock over a bunch of cans in the aisle she then calmly proceeded to the check-out to pay for her purchases. So after the women said this to my sister, my sister said she took the bag that she had packed the women's purchase in and turned in upside down throwing all of the items on the floor in front of the woman. Now mind you the Caucasian lady was upset but my sister said that she thought her stare was more intense than the other ladies, so she bagged her purchase, picked up her change, and left.

Chapter 3
Affirmative Action

It was the beginning of the 70s I had just moved out of the sixties my partner and myself "Chico & Buddy" had made a record that was widely played (I was astounded that ITunes had my record listed) it was entitled "A Thing Called The Jones" it was about the effects of heroin and the like in the black community (who brought the drugs into our community?), it's ironic that we still have a drug problem devastating our community. I reiterate with these Maximum/Minimum laws established by the Reagan and Bush administrations my son fell victim to its circumstance spending a ten year sentence in Federal Prison with no chance of parole even for good behavior. But if you want to talk about anything you fellows on the right, let's talk about the billion dollar a year prison system, the vending machine contracts, the uniform contracts, or the prisoners that run fish farms for a ludicrous minimum wage as the industry rakes in millions with slave labor cost at its core. Let's talk about the 19 million dollars a year that lobbyist pay the bought congress to enhance the prison system agenda. Let's talk about the more than 3,000 prisons in America both public and private. How better a nation would we be if 1,500 of those numbers juxtaposed the building of better schools for our children both black and white to be educated in. The CCA (Correction Corporation of American) generating approximately 200,000,000 million dollars a year off of the business of incarceration. Black men in prison might as well be sterile they aren't producing children to add to the population, is this a conspiracy is this their true intent? It is said that prison labor promotes 2.6 billion dollars in sales. It's not just about license plates now, even though inmates still make them. I thought the true and real purpose of prison was rehabilitation, but when an inmate comes home after serving his or her time satisfying the punishment that society has placed upon them they can't vote and we won't hire them, so what should they do? The same thing that initially put them in prison, I saw a movie once and as the inmate was leaving the prison the guard said to him see you in a few months, is that the purpose of all of this? Eleven million undocumented illegal's, 30,000 folk in Immigration Detention facilities. It seems to me that if you want to remain the majority you compromise the minority, duh. A lot of Americans can see this but this is not a true democracy anyway, the Founding Father's (former slave owners) didn't want it that way where the people would emphatically decide. If they told the story right they would stipulate that we are a Republic and with that form of government you have appointed representatives i.e., the Congress and other representative functionaries. So is that the reason in part for the vilification of the protesters that are out in force right now in our country, because the representatives who have been bought with a price won't allow it? I'm just a sixty-eight year old black man that has been an American all of his life, but I like a lot of other black American's are not stupid as to what we see, but what can we say in a true Republic? With that said as aforementioned it was the beginning of the 70s our record was making a little noise my record company bought us a 1971 Cadillac Eldorado Convertible I think the first issued by General Motors. How does the Force effect your driving I will tell you how, when a police officer stops you and the first thing out of his mouth is whose car is this, or how did you get this car. How many times I had to pop the hood as I watched police officers copy down the VIN number of the car without even mentioning my traffic oversight. My partner of blessed memory even went to jail one evening for back child support and his daughter was living with him and his wife had even been dead for a few years and never informed the courts, that discrepancy was handled after a night in jail. There was this elderly man living in Mt. Clemens he was a first class mentor that type of person that you knew wouldn't lead you wrong if only you would stop and just listen to him for a moment. Because that despised nomenclature "Affirmative Action" was in place to offer individuals who had suffered under the perpetual influences of the Force some help with employment, fair housing and other things under the auspices of our government. The folk on the right call it big government, I call it good government "because they helped Americans previously deprived, in fact still deprived." He informed me (while I was wearing a diamond stud in one ear and long processed hair) that Goodyear was hiring Retail Sales Managers and he had a connection with the store there in Mt. Clemens. I had explained to him that while I was in the service my M.O.S. was 71B30 (Senior Clerk Typist) in fact in my Quartermaster Battalion the 95th in Furth, Germany I was the only typist receiving Pro Pay, that meant I excelled in my job at sixty-eight I can still type about 80 wpm. I have worked in administration all of my life and I love it. So with those credentials he thought I would be a good candidate and he took me to the store, put in a good word for me and I was hired. I clicked from the start but some other white Store Managers with college degrees were mad so every now and then they would set me up to fail with account receivable questions or accounts payable questions, each Goodyear Store had their own profit and loss statement, etc., there was a black guy named George that was working for Goodyear who had a degree and he gave me a crash course on business acumen before he left the company he had gotten another offer and was moving on. I have always thought that I would have made George proud with how I used his instructions. I was tested again by my white counterparts but I passed the test to their dismay. I would eventually reach the ranks of Store Manager in record time, but the first store they gave me was really failing it had as the store manager an elderly Caucasian lady as its manager. I went in like a whirlwind put in TVs, appliances etc., in a store almost too small to hold them. I changed the mindset of the mechanics who before me were always bickering with one another. It came to me one evening that we spent eight waking hours together everyday and normally when we went home we would eat and either fall asleep on the couch and soon find ourselves in bed getting ready for the next day. I said to them we see each other and are around each other more awake time, than with our own families, couldn't we at least get along? A light bulb went off one of the mechanics said "Bill I never thought of it that way" it turned the Service Department around there commission checks got bigger and I was proud to be their boss. So with a record like that and the opportunity that Affirmative Action had afforded me to get my foot in the door my boss informed me that Goodyear was building a brand new store in Detroit and they wanted me to be the Manager, I was overwhelmed. This one story and I will move on. One day before I had even opened the store I was receiving tires and equipment on a daily basis because it was all spanking brand new. I will never forget that day, I was in the front of my store and the front door was opened and a white gentleman in a Brooks Brother suit, the quintessential wing tip shoes, and just the look of being a big executive came in. He walked up to the counter and told me his name of which I don't remember, he said that he was there to meet Bill Ferrell, I informed him that I was Bill Ferrell. He said that he had made a special trip to Detroit to meet me because he had heard so many fine things about me and he just wanted to meet the gentlemen that was causing them to build a $500,000 store for me to manage. That was a rewarding day all of the hard work had paid off and to this day I haven't forgotten that moment. After a few niceties he left my store and I have never to this day seen him again. My tenure at my store was successful I still have a bonus check on my wall in my home office for over $2,700.00 that I received the first year I was opened even though my store lost money, because of the new construction, we didn't lose as much as we could have because of the business that we generated, my ex (Dorothy) was really happy the day I brought that check home, $2,700.00 looked a little different in the70s than it does now. My tenure continued to flourish, I repeatedly won contest put on by our District Office and always beat a fellow colleague of Italian descent who managed a store in a community close to Detroit, and he would always come in second place. How shocked I was many years after I left Goodyear to run into my Italian friend at a hospital in Detroit his mother had taken ill and I was visiting a member from my church. As we parted I gave him one of my business cards he noticed that I was a minister and he gave me one of his cards. He was an executive for Goodyear working out of Akron, Ohio, back in the glory days all of the major tire companies Firestone etc., had headquarters in Akron. I hear he is now the head man for the state of Chicago. I thought to myself, well Bill they never would have promoted you to reach that level in Corporate America, but at least it let me know that I had the right stuff. As I conclude this chapter on Affirmative Action let me also show you how the Force affected me even during my time as a Store Manager with Goodyear. As aforementioned Affirmative Action allowed me to be hired by Goodyear with a High School Diploma, rather than a College Degree. For brevity sake a few examples. One year our District had experienced a very good year we were in the black and all was well. So as a reward for said productivity all the Store

Manager's in the state were invited for a weekend of golf etc., at Houghton Lake in Northern Michigan. The night I checked in I was placed in a room with a white store manager I do believe from Bay City, we exchanged greetings as we unpacked our luggage eventually leaving the room for the day's activities that were planned. Later that evening after supper I returned to my room and noticed my roommate was gone, initially I thought well he might have had a problem at his store or with his family to cause him to leave so abruptly. Before I retired for the evening there was a knock at my door it was my Jewish friend Don and he informed that the Store Manager didn't go back to Bay City he asked to be moved out of the room with me because he wasn't going to stay in a room with a black person (I'm being polite). I couldn't believe it because even with all that I'm writing I am not a prejudice person, I am just a person who wants to be received and respected as such. I told my friend that I couldn't believe that and he said don't worry Bill I'm changing my room and coming over here to your room, I told him that he didn't have to do that but he insisted because he felt ashamed about the whole fiasco. One other story from my Houghton Lake experience influenced by the Force. Since my friend was sharing the room with me that evening we talked awhile and he let me in on a few more goodies that I had no idea were going on. He said to me you know Bill whenever the District Manager holds a meeting for the Store Managers here in Michigan if you are not in attendance he tells off colored jokes and things that he doesn't say if you are there. I said "oh no" wow that's amazing. So for this 3-day weekend the next day was the scheduled golf day and after that a big dinner and awards presentation on the third day before going back to our perspective stores. Golf, what can I say I don't like it, the greens the out of doors, the manicured lawns I love but on that day we played 18 holes and me with no prior experience had to walk wherever I hit my ball. At the end of the day I hadn't walked that much when I served in the Army my legs were mush and the only 1 or 2 times that I did play after that encounter, I did with a cart and only played 9 holes. I have a friend (Larry Walker) who gave me a set of clubs and that couldn't get me out there again either. Back to Houghton, for those of you who may not know the objective of golf is to reach your hole in the least amount of strokes (each swing is a stroke). They set up the requirements for you to do that by establishing par for each hole, so if it is a par 4 you have to reach that hole in four strokes thereby making par, if you reach the hole in 3 strokes you birdie the hole and if you reach it in 2 strokes that's an eagle. All of this new found golf intelligence can be attributed to only one person Tiger Woods,

I have followed his career from the beginning and I'm glad he is coming back in line with the Tiger Woods I know his dad loved and influenced so much. I think this particular hole was a par 5 but it was elevated like up on a hill, so yours truly got to the hole. I hit the ball it went up the hill and over to the other side, I then went to the other side and hit the ball again it went to the other side, I kept going back and forth ending up with a 5 bogey in other words what should have caused me five strokes to do it took me ten. I was glad when that part of the outing was over for sure. Unbeknownst to me the next evening at a dinner with all of the Manager's from all over the State the same Store Manager's that had heard off color comments from the District Manager when I wasn't present. Our District Manager was from Texas and had that southern drawl that black folk have learned to be leery of until it is established if you are friend or foe. He called my name and he had a trophy in his hand (I said to myself I played horribly what am I getting a trophy for?) as I approached him he looked at the trophy and stated well, what does this say awarded to Bill Ferrell for the most strokes on one hole (that wasn't an award for greatness that was an award for failure, in golf circles for sure) well I'm pretty quick on my feet and as I reached for the trophy my District Manager said what happened on this hole Bill? I said well Mr. Harp I guess my ball couldn't understand Swahili there was a loud roar with all of the managers laughing, Mr. Harp's face turned beet red that was for all of his off colored jokes, and I walked back to my seat feeling satisfied with what I had done. On different occasions salesmen would come into my office and see that trophy with a golfer holding his club in the up position ready to swing, they would say oh you play golf? I would say with a certainty yep, hoping they wouldn't walk over and pick it up and notice the inscription would read "most strokes on one hole." Eventually my tenure with Goodyear would go awry it all started when we got a new District Manager whose reputation preceded him. He once challenged a black customer at a store he was managing and I heard that when the black man invited him outside, he went out with him and whipped the black man also. My store was right up there as far as generating capital I was always in close competition with our million dollar a year store off of Woodward Avenue in Detroit. But the day that the new District Manager finally visited my store I wasn't there. Eventually I was demoted; the auditor was brought in to find something on me I guess. If pilfering was going on it was due to some of my employees which was later proven. That is what corporations do they demote you in hopes of you quitting after leaving a prestigious position prior to that. I knew they wouldn't find anything and they didn't. I got a call from the District Office to meet with our new District Manager, I worked at a few different stores during my demotion (more on that later). When I got to Mr. Davis' office he apologized and said that I would be in line for another store as soon as one became available. But I had a question to ask Mr. Davis after getting his permission to do so; I informed him that I had heard he had made some inappropriate remarks about me before we had even met. He dropped his head and in a quiet voice admitted that he had. Right then the rubber that use to run through my veins according to my families depiction of me at the time, because I was all Goodyear. By him admitting that, it disheartened me and took away all of my fire. When I smell a rat I flee whether it was work, friendships, school, if something seems indifferent to me I will drop everything and just disappear. So Mr. Davis told me to go back to the store I was working at (the million dollar a year store) and he would contact me as soon as something was available. So I got back to the store where I was working with about 4 or 5 Retail Sales Manager Trainees, the position just under a Store Manager. One day after I got back from lunch on the little cubicle area that was mind I noticed that someone had very carefully used a newspaper to cut out letters and paste them to the sheet that hung before me and on this sheet were the words "Super Spook." I didn't say anything to my friend who managed the store just yet, but what I did do (I think they call it going into the zone now) was resurrect the Bill Ferrell that could sell anything to anybody. I generated about $6,000 in sales that day. The Store Manager would always go through all of the invoices at the end of the day to keep track of sales. It was then that I approached my friend who was white and Polish, he asked me what had happened to me that day he said you hit it like the old Bill I use to know. It was then that I showed him the note, he was livid he immediately got up and shut the whole store down (the front part that is) except for the service department they still worked on customer's cars. This meeting was for the sales staff only; Bob asked who wrote the note naturally no one came forth. He then went over the sales receipts for the day one manager did about $800, another manager did about $1,400., but no one except me went over $2,000. In fact I upped it by $4,000. Bob then told all of us that same fire that you saw in Bill Ferrell today is one of the reasons that he was the only black Store Manager in the state, he out performed everyone. I don't ever want to see the likes of this note again and if I ever find out who did it, I will fire you right there on the spot. About two weeks later I called my ex-during lunch and informed her I was leaving Goodyear, she concurred. Finally what Affirmative Action did do was to try and establish a level playing field, by affording the minority community an equal chance to the American Dream that we still haven't realized. I never will forget my boss calling me one day from the district office in a panic telling me to call any of my friends who I thought were worthy and offer them a job and career with Goodyear, the reason being the E.E.O.C. (The Equal Employment Opportunity Commission) had called him that morning stipulating that if Goodyear didn't hire more minorities they were going to pull the states tire contract with Goodyear. I did have one friend (Joe Young) to take advantage of the opportunity. The way I feel no wonder affirmative action was attacked it helped us (black folk). This is how I feel and a lot of other African American's also feel the same way because the Force causes that type of reaction, we can't blame everything on the Willy Lynch letter, there are varying forms of racism for sure depravation, lack of opportunity, impoverishment, unfair laws directed towards us and I could go on and on. You see anything that we have accomplished in America came through struggle or that particular white person with enough chutzpah to make things happen on our behalf. In a recent Jet article (2011) they noticed 10 laws that moved America, even with the effects of the Force present.

1. **Brown v. Board of Education 1954.** The unanimous Supreme Court decision ended segregation in public education—with mixed results. Rather than integrate, many public school systems shut down.
2. **Civil Rights, 1964 and Voting Rights Acts, 1965.** Without these laws, African-Americans would still be living in an Apartheid America.
3. **Medicare and Medicaid Acts, 1965.** The core pillars of America's social safety net provide essential access to health care for the elderly and poor.
4. **Head Start, 1965.** One of the most successful anti-poverty programs of the Great Society, it still provides free preschool to millions of low-income African-Americans.
5. **Affirmative Action, 1968.** Without it, the corridors of power and privilege would still be lily white and all male.
6. **Fair Housing Act, 1968.** Block-busting real estate agents and redlining banks no longer police the boundaries of White Neighborhoods. Still, silent covenants fuel residential segregation.

7. **Title IX, 1972..** Young girls can now aspire and compete to become elite professional athletes.
8. **Omnibus Crime Bill, 1994.** Mass incarceration under this law decimated Black communities.
9. **Personal responsibility and Work Opportunity Reconciliation Act, 1996.** Welfare-to-work pushed people off government assistance after five years but has never addressed the underlying racial disparity in employment and opportunity.
10. **Patient Protection and Affordable Care Act, 2010.** President Obama's health reform provides coverage to more than 30 million formerly uninsured Americans.

Black Folk Stop Killing One Another We Need To Unify!

All of the above laws have been repealed, or continually vilified.

Chapter 4
Conclusion and Solutions

As I move towards completion I want to note a few things. In a speech given on September 9th, 2006 at Salt Lake City, Utah.

By Dr. Daneen G. Peterson, PhD[2]., entitled:

"America is a Constitutional Republic....Not a Democracy"

And I quote "How often have you heard people refer to America as a Democracy? When was the last time that you heard America referred to as a Republic? There is a very good reason that our Pledge of Allegiance refers to our country as a Republic and there is a very good reason that our Declaration of Independence and our constitution do not even mention the word "democracy". Many people are under the false impression our form of government is a democracy, or representative democracy. This is of course completely untrue. The Founders were extremely knowledgeable about the issue of democracy and feared a democracy as much as a monarchy. They understood that the only entity that can take away the people's freedom is their own government, either by being too weak to protect them from external threats or by

[2] Speech given by Dr. Daneen G. Peterson, Ph.D at Salt Lake City, Utah September 9, 2006 "America is a Constitutional Republic…Not a Democracy

becoming too powerful and taking over every aspect of life. They knew very well the meaning of the word "democracy", and the history of democracies; and they were deliberately doing everything in their power to prevent having a democracy. In a Republic, the sovereignty resides with the people themselves. In a Republic, one may act on his own or through his representatives when he chooses to solve a problem. The people have no obligation to the government; instead, the government is a servant of the people, and obliged to its owner, We the People. Many politicians have lost sight of that fact. A Constitutional Republic has some similarities to democracy in that it uses democratic processes to elect representatives and pass new laws, etc. The critical difference lies in the fact that a Constitutional Republic has a Constitution that limits the powers of the government. It also spells out how the government is structured, creating checks on its power and balancing power between the different branches.

The goal of a Constitutional Republic was to avoid the dangerous extreme of either tyranny or mobocracy but what exists in America today is a far cry from the Constitutional Republic our forefathers brought forth. Today we have a mobocracy occurring in our streets all across America. Sadly, such mobocracy or 'mob rule' was endorsed and encouraged by Sen. John McCain who praised the recent wave of pro-illegal immigration demonstrations by saying...."if the protesters hang tough they will succeed in forcing Congress to liberalize immigration laws. If such demonstrations continue, I think we will have a bill for the President to sign soon....The more debate, the more demonstrations, the more likely we will prevail.' He was of course referring to the Senate's massive illegal-alien amnesty bill S. 2611 which did in fact, pass. Was S. 2611 passed to appease the mob? If so, it is a perfect example of rule by mobocracy!

Article IV Section 4 of the Constitution states: "The United States shall guarantee to every State in this Union a Republican form of Government, and shall protect each of them against invasion....Not only is our Constitution being ignored, the exact OPPOSITE is being encouraged by John McCain and seconded by ALL those who voted for S. 2611 in the Senate. If you want to preserve the Constitutional Republic you should vote out of office.....every single senator that voted for S.2611. "Un-Quote"

I thought this information would enlighten my African American brothers and sisters and interest that whiner on the right that has a talk show in the evening on 760 AM. As I look at the situation in Washington I am so sick of the catch words these guys use on the right, Socialist (to mean they don't want government to take care of anyone) but all of my adult life I have seen these folk in Washington send money by the bushel baskets to help the world community and no one complains or at least they didn't in the past that is before the Force went into effect relative to my President. Although there is money going to Haiti and some parts of Africa because of the Force their infrastructure is still lacking God bless folk like Oprah Winfrey, Sean Penn, Angeline Jolie and Brad Pitt to name a few that are really out there helping those in the minority and also Diane Sawyer for her coverage.......but I still find Haiti and Africa lacking in the big scheme of things. What would happen if some of these Senators didn't have decent drinking water, lights to light up their gated communities, or if they had to go outside to the bathroom what would they do, they haven't the slightest idea? While they are passing bills to deny the 99% they ought to put one in place that requires all Senators to live as their constituents live to garner a better understanding of whom they represent and serve. Another word that ticks me off is Activist they mean it in a negative way, but to me it means an individual that is brave enough to stand up for what is rightly theirs, a piece of the American Dream. During earlier times in the South there was always that one black person that took no mess from the Klan or anyone else if you tried to rub him the wrong way it wouldn't be pretty. Folk like that used to be called crazy, "don't mess with old Joe over the hill he's crazy." Joe wasn't crazy all he wanted was some respect and he wouldn't accept anything less, activist Joe. The land that black folk lost in the South due to shady deals, thievery, and murder is too great to comment on, who took the land, who played the tricks, who cheated us, what do you call them activist or crooks? I choose to call them the latter and I'm not budging. Also my Webster Dictionary says of socialism: "Any of various economic and political theories advocating collective or governmental ownership and administration of the means of production and distribution of goods. A system of society or group living in which there is no private property. A system or condition of society in which the means of production are owned and controlled by the state. A stage of society in Marxist theory transitional between capitalism and communism and distinguished by unequal distribution of goods and pay according to work done." It seems to me that some parts of this definition apply to our Congress and not my President…….who is holding up production. Can we own our property in America? I ask who messed up the housing sector, not my President, I'll give you a hint it starts with Wall. Nothing here about NAFTA, my President didn't do that, nor did he let China buy our debt a lot of folks understand that, so that makes it more and more intolerable to hear the rhetoric on a daily basis like we are all stupid. Webster also says of the word activist: A doctrine or practice that emphasizes direct vigorous action especially in support of or opposition to one side of a controversial issue. Hum, controversial issue second class citizenship nawwww, forty-acres and a mule nawwww, reparations nawwww, improper voting practices nawwww, infant mortality, lack of proper medical care, high incarceration nawwww, red-lining, high insurance premiums, schools with no books and other opportunities nawwww, credit issues nawwww, profiling, maximum minimum sentences for certain drugs nawwww, I'm sure I could go on and on in a country that the Force controls. I will only say that relative to the aforementioned controversial issues I would surely love to have some type of representation to level the playing field, so to me activist is not a negative connotation. I was appalled to hear a Senator or Senator's repeatedly use the word activism in a negative format. If they have that certain drawl in their dialect I'm immediately leery until they show me whether they are friend or foe by their actions. This Senator referred to Justice Thurgood Marshall negatively as such, and a lot of folks took umbrage with his statements, because Justice Marshall is held in high esteem for his standing up for the downtrodden in our society. You also hear a negative connotation relative to Liberation Theology as if it is a bad thing; Jesus came to this planet to set the captives free (do any of these Senator's go to church?). The poor will always be with us, but what they don't seem to understand that it is better to give than receive. If I were them I would be more concerned with the "you reap what you sow part." See if Justice Marshall was negligent in his speech. This speech Thurgood Marshall gave in 1987 was part of the constitutional bicentennial celebration. Politicians and Judges around the country were praising the "Founding Fathers" for their genius at writing a document that established the guiding legal principles of the republic for generations. But **Marshall was one of the few voices pointing out that the original constitution required numerous amendments and came to a crisis that required a Civil War to solve**. In a time of flag waving and patriotic rhetoric, Marshall's comments surprised many and created Front-page headlines: Remarks of Thurgood Marshall at the Annual Seminar of the SAN FRANCISCO PATENT AND TRADEMARK LAW ASSOCIATION in Maui, Hawaii May 6, 1987[3] 1987 marks the 200th anniversary of the United States Constitution. A Commission has been established to coordinate the celebration. The official meetings, essay contests, and festivities had begun. The

---

[3] Speech given by Justice Thurgood Marshall at the Annual Seminar of the San Francisco Patent and Trademark Law Association in Maui, Hawaii May 6, 1987.

planned commemoration will span three years, and I am told 1987 is "dedicated to the memory of the Founders and the document they drafted in Philadelphia." We are to "recall the achievements of our Founders and the knowledge and experience that inspired them, the nature of the government they established, its origins, its character, and its ends, and the rights and privileges of citizenship, as well as its attendant responsibilities."

Like many anniversary celebrations, the plan for 1987 takes particular events and holds them up as the source of all the very best that has followed. Patriotic feelings will surely swell, prompting proud proclamations of the wisdom, foresight, and sense of justice shared by the Framers and reflected in a written document now yellowed with age. This is unfortunate not the patriotism itself, but the tendency for the celebration to oversimplify, and overlook the many other events that have been instrumental to our achievements as a nation. The focus of this celebration invites a complacent belief that the vision of those who debated and compromised in Philadelphia yielded the "more perfect Union" it is said we now enjoy. I cannot accept this invitation, for I do not believe that the meaning of the Constitution was forever "fixed" at the Philadelphia Convention. Nor do I find the wisdom, foresight, and sense of justice exhibited by the Framers particularly profound. To the contrary, the government they devised was defective from the start, requiring several amendments, a civil war, and momentous social transformation to attain the system of constitutional government, and its respect for the individual freedoms and human rights, we hold as fundamental today. When contemporary Americans cite "The Constitution," they invoke a concept that is vastly different from what the Framers barely began to construct two centuries ago. For a sense of the evolving nature of the Constitution we need look no further than the first three words of the document's preamble: 'We the People." When the Founding Fathers used this phrase in 1787; they did not have in mind the majority of America's citizens. "We the People" included, in the words of the Framers, "the whole Number of free Persons." On a matter as basic as the right to vote, for example, Negro slaves were excluded, although they were counted for representational purposes at three fifths each. Women did not gain the right to vote for over a hundred and thirty years. These omissions were intentional. The record of the Framers' debates on the slave question is especially clear: The Southern States acceded to the demands of the New England States for giving Congress broad power to regulate commerce, in exchange for the right to continue the slave trade. The economic interests of the regions coalesced: New Englanders engaged in the "carrying trade" would profit from transporting slaves from Africa as well as goods produced in America by slave labor. The perpetuation of slavery ensured the primary source of wealth in the Southern States. Despite this clear understanding of the role slavery would play in the new republic, use of the words "slaves" and "slavery" was carefully avoided in the original document. Political representation in the lower House of Congress was to be based on the population of "free Persons" in each State, plus three fifths of all "other Persons." Moral principles against slavery, for those who had them, were compromised, with no explanation of the conflicting principles for which the American Revolutionary War had ostensibly been fought: the self-evident truths "that all men are created equal, that they are endowed by their Creator with certain unalienable Rights, that among these are Life, Liberty and the pursuit of Happiness." It was not the first such compromise. Even these ringing phrases from the Declaration of Independence are filled with irony, for an early draft of what became that Declaration assailed the King of England for suppressing legislative attempts to end the slave trade and for encouraging slave rebellions. The final draft adopted in 1776 did not contain this criticism. And so again at the Constitutional Convention eloquent objections to the institution of slavery went unheeded, and its opponents eventually consented to a document which laid a foundation for the tragic events that were to follow. Pennsylvania's Governor Morris provides an example. He opposed slavery and the counting of slaves in determining the basis for representation in Congress. At the Convention he objected that "The inhabitant of Georgia [or] South Carolina who goes to the coast of Africa, and in defiance of the most sacred laws of humanity tears away his fellow creatures from their dearest connections and damns them to the most cruel bondages, shall have more votes in a Government instituted for protection of the rights of mankind, than the Citizen of Pennsylvania or New Jersey who views with a laudable horror, so nefarious a Practice." And yet Governor Morris eventually accepted the three fifths accommodation. In fact, he wrote the final draft of the Constitution, the very document the bicentennial will commemorate. As a result of compromise, the right of the southern States to continue importing slaves was extended, officially, at least until 1808. We know that it actually lasted a good deal longer, as the Framers possessed no monopoly on the ability to trade moral principles for self-interest. But they nevertheless set an unfortunate example. Slaves could be imported, if the commercial interests of the North were protected. To make the 50 compromise even more palatable, customs duties would be imposed at up to ten dollars per slave as a means of raising public revenues. No doubt it will be said, when the unpleasant truth of the history of slavery in America is mentioned during this bicentennial year, that the Constitution was a product of its times, and embodied a compromise which, under other circumstances, would not have been made. But the effects of the Framers' compromise have remained for generations. They arose from the contradiction between guaranteeing liberty and justice to all, and denying both to Negroes. The original intent of the phrase, "We the People," was far too clear for any ameliorating construction. Writing for the Supreme Court in 1857, Chief Justice Taney penned the following passage in the Dred Scott case, on the issue whether, in the eyes of the Framers, slaves were "constituent members of the sovereignty," and was to be included among "We the People": "We think they are not, and that they are not included, and were not intended to be included.... They had for more than a century before been regarded as beings of an inferior order and altogether unfit to associate with the white race...; and so far inferior, that they had no rights which the white man was bound to respect; and that the Negro might justly and lawfully be reduced to slavery for his benefit.... [A]accordingly, a Negro of the African race was regarded ... as an article of property, and held, and bought and sold as such.... [N]o one seems to have doubted the correctness of the prevailing opinion of the time." And so, nearly seven decades after the Constitutional Convention, the Supreme Court reaffirmed the prevailing opinion of the Framers regarding the rights of Negroes in America. It took a bloody civil war before the l3th Amendment could be adopted to abolish slavery, though not the consequences slavery would have for future Americans. While the Union survived the civil war, the Constitution did not. In its place arose a new, more promising basis for justice and equality, the 14th Amendment, ensuring protection of the life, liberty, and property of all persons against deprivations without due process, and guaranteeing equal protection of the laws. And yet almost another century would pass before any significant recognition was obtained of the rights of black Americans to share equally even in such basic opportunities as education, housing, and employment, and to have their votes counted, and counted equally. In the meantime, blacks joined America's military to fight its wars and invested untold hours working in its factories and on its farms, contributing to the development of this country's magnificent wealth and waiting to share in its prosperity. What is striking is the role legal principles have played throughout America's history in determining the condition of Negroes. They were enslaved by law, emancipated by law, disenfranchised and segregated by law; and, finally, they have begun to win equality by law. Along the way, new constitutional principles have emerged to meet the challenges of a changing society. The progress has been dramatic, and it will continue. The men who gathered in Philadelphia in 1787 could not have envisioned these changes. They could not have imagined, nor would they have accepted, that the document they were drafting would one day be construed by a Supreme Court to which had been appointed a woman and the descendent of an African slave. We the People" no longer enslave, but the credit does not belong to the Framers. It belongs to those who refused to acquiesce in outdated notions of "liberty," "justice," and "equality," and who strived to better themselves. And so we must be careful, when focusing on the events which took place in Philadelphia two centuries ago, that we not overlook the momentous events which followed, and thereby lose our proper sense of perspective. Otherwise, the odds are that for many Americans the bicentennial celebration will be little more than a blind pilgrimage to the shrine of the original document now stored in a vault in the National Archives. If we seek, instead, a sensitive understanding of the Constitution's inherent defects, and its promising evolution through 200 years of history, the celebration of the "Miracle at Philadelphia" will, in my view, be a far more meaningful and humbling experience. We will see that the true miracle was not the birth of the Constitution, but its life, a life nurtured through two turbulent centuries of our own making, and a life embodying much good fortune that was not. Thus, in this bicentennial year, we may not all participate in the festivities with flag waving fervor. Some may more quietly commemorate the suffering, struggle, and sacrifice that have triumphed over much of what was wrong with the original document, and observe the anniversary with hopes not realized and promises not fulfilled. I plan to celebrate the bicentennial of the Constitution as a living document, including the Bill of Rights and the other amendments protecting individual freedoms and human rights. So should the term activist be applied to such a wonderful and true speech as this? I say no. What the justice was doing was addressing a deficit in the constitution that needed to be addressed now at the time it may or may not have been controversial but it is still an issue of concern. I have never and will never think of myself as $3/5^{th}$ of a human being I'm all human and made in the image of my creator and not some damn monkey. I had a professor in seminary Dr. Zimmerman, he talked about the similarity of design, white folk have two ears, black folk have two ears, white folk have two arms, black folk have two arms also, white folk have two eyes, black folk have two eyes, you get my point unlike my experience in Germany with the Fraulein looking for my tail, if I did have a tail and white folk didn't there would be a difference. But we are all related to each other through the power of our creation by our creator. Regardless to whether you wanted to accept my blood in a transfusion, when I use to donate to the Red Cross in my youth no one was rejected based upon their skin color but only on the redness of their blood, similarity in design. Lastly, I was looking at a movie the other day entitled "Inside Job". It was a presentation to amplify the breakdown of the financial system in America and its cause, two things came to mind initially. How Mr. Gingrich ducked when he heard a heckler, I've seen that type of duck in real life and trust me I know exactly how it looks. Then I thought about this movie and the interviewing of all these fat wall-street cats in their thousand dollar tailored suits being ever cautious and not answering anything with substance. One of them was so arrogant that he told the interviewer you only have another three minutes and I'm done with this interview. Some of these guys haven't done any time at all. Like that arrogant BP executive after they had messed up the Gulf talking about the "little people." Like that one Wall Street executive that had his own private elevator that went to his top floor office without coming in contact with anyone,

I just saw the movie Tower Heist and it had somewhat of the same scenario to its theme. I wonder how these civil intellectuals would act in a cell with someone named "Snake," would they show that same arrogance, I think not. A gentleman of Chinese descent said something very interesting at the end of the Inside Job movie of (which I recommend others to view). Like that movie on Bush when the interviewer was interviewing some firm that had generated a list of over 20,000 people who were felons that couldn't vote. One of the people was a veteran of the wars in place now and stated that he had never been to jail in his life, that person went in his office and closed the door refusing to answer any more questions. It is so blatantly obvious what these folk are doing and what they are made of, the Bible says that the "Love of Money is the Root of all Evil" there is a lot of evil out there, God help us. The Chinese gentleman, he felt it unfair that Financial Engineers make four to 100 times more than an engineer who builds bridges he further stated that a financial engineer builds dreams and when those dreams become nightmares other people pay, Amen. I think there is a generation problem in Congress I catch flack from my own family arguing about the values I was raised on. I've often said all of my kids would be in Foster Care with this abuse sensitivity; my family did not spare the rod trust me. When I went in the Army in 63, those Drill Sergeants would put their hands on you and I mean that literally, one Sergeant kicked a fellow soldier in the rear because he continually got out of step you can't do that now. How many times did I have to go to my counselor's office in Junior High School, he was a bigggggg German gentleman named Hoffelmeyer, he would have me bend over his desk and he had this paddle with holes in it and he would give me two swift firm licks and send me back to my class many a times with my rear end burning. Discipline has it place and as my former pastor has said he believes there is a direct correlation between the head and your rear end, in other words if you tap that rear end right the head will follow suit. I know there are many that don't agree with me, but I never understood it until I got to be an adult. Then I realized what my father meant when he spanked me, he said he did it because he loved me, I always thought Dad if you love me why are you spanking me? Now at sixty-eight I appreciate those spankings because he gave them to me rather than someone in the streets that didn't have any compassionate connection to me. Some of these guys can't get over my President, they remember a time that all we did was bring them drinks, make them laugh, open our eyes real big and speak with a broken brogue, fellows those days are gone and they aren't coming back. Many a black family as my mentor Dr. Anthony C. Campbell once said were "raised on stuff that other folk threw away. What do I mean there was a time that slaughter houses would give away pig feet, pig ears, chitterlings, pig heads (head cheese), pig tail, even ox-tails, etc.., Then our parents would go home and cook that food which gave us strength and watch many a black youth go on to higher heights making their parents proud on the stuff that other folk threw away. Then all of a sudden, the man saw this and put a price on everything and it's not that cheap anymore, we'll eat beans everyday, catch our fish and hunt if need be to feed our families fellows on the right. We are entrenched and aren't going anywhere we will not be defeated. Look at our history we are survivors. Yes we are still treated like we are second class citizens, but you realized that through the advent of unions and the fairness agenda of Henry Ford paying all of his employees $5.00 an hour when it was unheard of. You are so conniving and pernicious that you want to destroy the middle class and have no concern if you hurt your own race in doing so, just to get at us. But we aren't stupid we have our eyes on you just like you have your eyes on us. I really wonder if any of these guys go to church or if they do, are they awake during the sermon or asleep? I had a catholic friend of African descent who belongs to a Catholic church in a wealthy suburb outside the metropolitan area of Detroit and he told me that on the 1st Sunday of each year, the one per centers would come to church and right a pledge check to cover the whole years dues and wouldn't come back to church again until the next first Sunday of the next year. I guess it's true that it would be easier for a rich person likened to a camel (or rope *"gamla"* in Aramaic) to go through an eye of a needle than a rich man getting into heaven. When one pursues only money there focus is taken off of God and his "better to give than receive ideology." All of the brylcreem (a little dab will do you!) senators need to go and be replaced with younger members of this generation their time has passed and it is not coming back no matter what they try to do, we as a people (African Americans) are entrenched we our Americans and we aren't going anywhere. Our congress ought to look like the face of America and what it is supposed to stand for, Chinese, Korean, Native-American, Arabs, Africans, Indians, Jews and Gentiles alike America is losing its whiteness and that is driving some folk bananas. You reap what you sew, my mother use to say "if you dig a hole for someone else to fall in, you had better dig it big enough for two folk, because what you put out will also come back and get you, but I might be out of place you learn that if you go to church. In an article by John Solomon a Washington Post Staff Writer January 20, 2007 he talked about the new rules that still allowed Congress many perks. It stated in part that voters in the last election demanded a change in Washington's ethics climate. The new Democratic congressional leadership responded with sweeping new prohibitions on gifts and travel from lobbyists, tough new limits on once-cheap corporate jet flights for lawmakers, and new requirements that lawmakers disclose the pet projects they earmark. But the new rules, the toughest changes since Watergate, still leave lots of room for special interests to curry favor and lawmakers to raise big dollars. Congress itself imposes the ethics rules upon itself. I wish I could do that with my annual COLA, vote for the type of insurance coverage that I want, vote who can or cannot give me money and how to hide it if need be (current rules for Corporations and their giving of money towards the outcome of elections). He further states in the article lawmakers can still go to widely attended events or campaign events and accept freebies such as meals (is anybody hungry out there if you get free food its Socialism). The real truth is this; White Americans receive 34% of Food Stamps, 22% to Black Americans and 17% to Hispanics. I reached back into my archives and found this Ebony (African America's Magazine you ought pick up a copy Mr. Beck you might learn more about us) article from December 1992 issue entitled "Who

Gets Welfare? Despite Prevailing[4] Stereotype, Whites, not Blacks, Collect the Greatest Share of Public Aid Dollars it states "Say the word "welfare" and immediately the image of the lazy Black welfare queen who breeds for profit surfaces in the minds of those who have come to believe the hideous stereotype." It is a myth that persists despite government figures and authoritative studies showing that Whites overwhelmingly reap the lion's share of the dole. The image of the Black "welfare cheat," the notion, they say, comes from society's resentment of seemingly able bodied people getting paid for doing nothing. "For some people, there is a need to believe that there are professional welfare recipients who are deliberately trying to get not only what they need to survive, but more," says Anne D. Hill, director of programs for the National Urban League. People say to themselves: "I work. How come this person who appears to be healthy isn't working?" We tend to equate our condition with others without fully knowing their circumstances. Hill and other welfare supporters argue that numbers, and not erroneous stereotypes, tell the real story about public assistance clients: Some 61 percent of welfare recipients are White, while 33 percent are Black, according to 1990 Census Bureau statistics,

---

[4] Article from Ebony Magazine December 1992 issue entitled "Who gets welfare?" Despite prevailing stereotype, whites, not blacks, collect greatest share of public aid dollars.

the latest figures available. (According to the Wiki Answer website and based on the 2006 population of each respective race in the United States, it is: 37.8% of the white population is on welfare, 27.78% of the black population is on welfare and 11.47% of the Hispanic population is on welfare). The federal government defines welfare as all entitlement programs funded through taxes. These programs, listed as "direct benefit payments for individuals" by the Office of Management and Budget, make up $730 billion or 43 percent of the $1.47 trillion the government will spend this fiscal year." So the lies that these folk on the right are generating relative to their fear of our using these entitlements unfairly in fact applies more so to their race than ours, get it right fellows, get it right! A final look again at some of the perks of Congress. "Nonprofit organizations and universities can still provide lawmakers free travel in many cases. And lawmakers can still offer creative opportunities for special interest to meet with them – for a price. Senator Max Baucus the new chairman of the tax-writing Senate Finance Committee is offering special interests a chance next month to go skiing and snowmobiling in Big Sky country. All it takes is a $2,000 donation per person or a $5.000 donation from a political action committee, according to a "Save the Date" solicitation his Glacier PAC sent out to lobbyists. If lobbyists miss the first outing; they can still catch Baucus this summer for fly-fishing or horseback riding at "Camp Baucus," the invitation promises. "It makes one pause when members of Congress raise one hand to vote on an ethics proposal to limit special interests and with the other hand outstretched behind their back ask for campaign contributions or perks from special interests." Said Kent Cooper, a former federal election regulator who studies ethics and political money. I'm trying to show a pattern here, when former Senator Trent Lott (R-Miss) was selected in November to be the new GOP whip, he flew with a company lobbyist aboard BellSouth's corporate Jet from Washington to Jackson, Miss. The senator and lobbyist got to know each other better, discussed religion and talked generally about BellSouth's merger with AT&T that was pending at the Federal Communications Commission, company spokesman Bill MCCloskey said. A few weeks later, Lott was the highest-ranking lawmaker to sign a Dec. 8th letter in which 14 senators demanded that the FCC approved the BellSouth – AT&T merger before the end of the holidays. Regulators approved the deal on the eve of New Year's weekend. I need a lobbyist to help me with my Medicaid that was just taken away from me after losing my wife in June of 2011, I lost $800.00 out of my monthly income (my wife received Medicaid based upon our old salary). I went from

$2,220.00 a month for two people to $1,400.00 for myself but my Medicaid was cancelled because I make too much money, I reiterate I need a lobbyist to get my Medicaid back and I don't even want to go on a trip, how's that. At the end of the article he gave this illustration of two more representatives, Rep. John T. Doolittle (R-Calif) and Rep. Alan B. Mollohan (D-W.Va). He stated that one area that was not addressed in the new rules was the use of campaign funds that can directly or indirectly benefit lawmakers or their families. Doolittle drew the scrutiny of federal investigators during the Jack Abramoff lobbying scandal when it came out that the congressman's wife was getting paid both by Abramoff and by Doolittle's political action committee for fundraising work around the same time the congressman took actions favorable to Abramoff's clients. Reports Doolittle filed with the Federal Election Commission show his Superior California Federal Leadership PAC paid his wife's firm nearly $100,00 during the 2000 election cycle, including $4,000 in the weeks after the November election. Doolittle has said he will no longer apply his wife that way. Likewise, Mollohan reported that in the last two months of 2006 his campaign spent $140,000 on lawyers he had hired to deal with his legal problems. Mollohan was forced to step down from the House ethics committee last year over a federal probe into taxpayer money he steered to a network of nonprofit foundations connected to him or other insiders. "The love of money is the root of all evil." (Added by me). No wonder you can't run for office if you are broke, the campaign money you raise can be used for all sorts of things, I personally feel money has no place in politics (don't I sound stupid!!!) but no one wants to hear that for sure, that would be too much like right. Another article posted by DC Republican in Strange Congress on Feb 17th, 2009 stated with so much talk on Capitol Hill about the need for capping the perks and salaries afforded to executives of companies who are seeking federal dollars, I thought that it would be interesting to explore some of the perks that are received by those who not only seek, but spend our hard earned dollars: Members of Congress.

Free parking: Not only do members of Congress receive parking on Capitol Hill, but they also receive free (prime) private parking spots at the two nearby airports, Reagan National and Dulles airport.

Salary: The current salary for a member of Congress is $174,000. However, Congress has the authority to raise their salary as they wish, without having to hold a vote. (I wish all Social Security recipients had that same power, all in favor of that applying to us signify by the raising of your hand) comment added. It's also interesting to note that during the great depression, members of Congress voluntarily took a pay cut. I somehow don't think we'll see that happen these days.

Perks from Lobbyists: Despite a slew of ethics regulations regarding gifts from lobbyists, Members of Congress are still able to use their lobbyist ties to get into events that regular people simply do not have access to. For example, if a Member of Congress wanted a prime ticket to a sold-out-event, he could still get that ticket from lobbyists he's close with, as long as the face value of the ticket is reimbursed by the Member.

However, this money doesn't have to come from the Member's pocket, but instead can come from the usually deep campaign account, which usually contains money from lobbyists and their associated PACs.

Days Off: While most Americans get one day off for Memorial Day and sometimes Presidents Day, members of Congress get the entire week off. However, Congress doesn't like to call these vacation days, but instead call them "District Work Periods," even though there is nothing requiring them to be in their district during those times. Congress also gets a number of additional recesses, some lasting as long as a month.

Additional perks of being in Congress, all paid for by you, the taxpayer (from NTU):

- Comfortable salaries that are often determined through legislative sleight-of-hand. Contrary to the arguments of many Washington "insiders," the cost of living has rarely eroded the historical value of lawmakers' pay, which on a constant dollar basis is hovering near the postwar high.
- Pension benefits that are two to three times more generous than those offered in the private sector for similarly-salaried executives. Taxpayers directly cover at least 80 percent of this costly plan. Congressional pensions are also inflation protected a feature that fewer than 1 in 10 private plans offer.
- Health and life insurance, approximately ¾ and ⅓ of whose costs, respectively, are subsidized by taxpayers.
- Travel to far-flung destinations as well as to home states and districts. Despite recent attempts to toughen gift and travel rules, "junkets" are still readily available prerogatives for many Members.
- A wide range of smaller perks that have defied reform efforts, from cut-rate health clubs to fine furnishings.

- The franking privilege, which gives lawmakers millions in tax dollars to create a favorable public image. Experts across the political spectrum have labeled the frank as an unfair electioneering tool. In past election cycles, Congressional incumbents have spent as much on f ranking alone as challengers have spent on their entire campaigns.
- An office staff that performs "constituent services" and doles out pork barrel spending, providing more opportunities for "favors" that can be returned only at election time.
- Exemptions and immunities from tax, pension, and other laws that burden private citizens – all crafted by lawmakers themselves.

Death Dues: Even if a lawmaker was to become the ninth member of Congress killed in a plane crash while in office, generous benefits would be awarded to his or her family. The families of current members of Congress who die typical receive a full year's salary (as reiterated when my wife passed I lost $800.00 out of my monthly income and almost sunk, also I only got $255.00 from Social Security towards her burial) comment added.....as compensation. Survivors of Representatives are entitled to an additional sum. That amounts to at least $174,000 for rank and file legislators, and more for those in leadership positions. It's not unusual for death benefits to be paid to the relatives of people who die while working for the government; what's surprising is the scope of the benefits for lawmakers. By comparison, the families of members of the armed forces killed on the battlefield in Iraq or Afghanistan are only entitled to $100,000 for their loss.

Boehner Benefits

No legislator – living or dead – has been paid a higher salary by the taxpayer than Speaker Boehner.

While in office, the Ohio Republican will get the top annual salary in Congress $223,500. His Senate counterpart, Majority Leader Harry Reid, D – Nev., and other congressional leaders are paid much less, $193,400 per year. The House speaker's taxpayer-funded perks don't stop when he leaves office. Like all members of Congress who have held office for at least five years – Boehner has been in the House since 1991 – he is entitled to a generous pension. But Boehner gets an additional benefit: Up to $1 million per year for up to five years after he leaves the office to "facilitate the administration, settlement and conclusion of matters pertaining to or arising out of" his tenure as speaker of the

House, according to a little known law. This provision has allowed former Speaker Denny Hastert, R -0- Ill., to rack up more than $997,000 during the course of three years to document materials related to his time in office. "The archiving continues to go on," spokesman Brad Hahn told the *Chicago Tribune* in Feb. 2010. "I wouldn't want to speculate on a timeline." This is a far cry from the Representatives of Congress at the start from 1789 – 1995 they were paid $6 per day no limit, a lot different from $174,000 received in 2011. How can these Congressmen with a clear mind do what they do to the American taxpayer who supplies the funds to the Government to be abused by the same government, it makes no sense. Like the recent interest in the Iowa Caucus, the Iowa Caucus means nothing to me where the vote is 97% white, that's not a true representation of America, hypothetically it might be but literally speaking it's not. In a recent article in the Jackson Advocate by contributive editor Ivory Phillips entitled "Which America will survive the current civil war"? One thing for sure white folk are buying up all the guns, I heard a newsman say that it was probably for self-defense, against who or what the Force? He states in his article, "Although it has not been openly declared, there is a war going on in America. It is not a shooting war, but it is a war nevertheless. On one side are mostly conservatives;

(Iowa) on the other, liberals. One side is made up primarily of early arriving European groups. The other is made up of later arrivals. The war is basically a cultural one, utilizing the media, the pulpit, the podium, and public offices. Unless a solution is soon found, the country will be rent asunder. It is a problem[5] that has been escalating rapidly for the last thirty years.

Nevertheless, it is the very nature of what the United States of America was declared itself to be in the Declaration of Independence. After that declaration, it was re-stated in the First Amendment of the Constitution, the Gettysburg Address, and the American Creed and on the base of the Statute of Liberty. America was to be open to all persons desiring the blessings of liberty. It was not to be the province of any particular linguistic, religious, racial or ethnic group. It was to be the land of the free and the home of the brave. It turns out that these lofty pronouncements were either hypocritical or represented a much more difficult task than was realized. The U.S.A. had a diverse origin. Although the dominant group in the country was European and Christian, there were free African people, (whose history has never been reported properly I relate to an old African Proverb that states, "Until Lions Tell Their Tale, The Story Of The Hunt Will

---

[5] Article written by Contributing Editor Ivory Phillips in the latter part of 2011 entitled "Which America will survive the current civil war?

Always Glorify The Hunter" this book is my lion's tale) comment added….native Americans, Jews, and a sprinkling of Asians and Middle Easterners in the country. As the European Christian majority grew in economic and political power, its language, economic system, political structures, educational system, theological and moral perspectives, and legal framework became the standards. The process of Americanization meant adopting the white, Christian models. (Greco/Roman) comment added…. The more we see this occurring the more we see America's base being narrowed; the more we see other groups being marginalized. This is generally what happened from the 1800s through the 1960s. It was almost seen as a natural process by the dominant group. Then as the demographics of the country rapidly changed over the last 50 years, the division between the old line white Christian majority and the rising group of other people has become deeper, escalating the cultural war that we see today. Especially since the election of Barack Obama as President, the people who feel that America is and should remain a country based upon European, Christian principles and foundations have felt under attack and that they must stand and hold the line, lest America be lost (The Force) comment added…..On the other hand, many people of other faiths, other moral and theological persuasions, and other ethnicities have felt not only marginalized but attacked as being un-American. For us the question then, becomes can America become the country dreamed of in such lofty documents as the "Declaration of Independence." The writer would suggest that honest politicians and sincere voters carefully read the First Amendment's Establishment or Freedom of Conscience Clause, which says, "Congress shall make no law respecting an establishment of religion" and its Free Exercise Clause, which says, "or prohibiting the free exercise thereof," what the Supreme Court has said about these clauses over the last 50 years; and then, reflect upon the core moral teaching of some of history's greatest teachers, The essence of the First Amendment is that people of authority in public positions or working for public agencies are forbidden from saying or doing anything that promotes any religion and the idea of religion; and by the same token people in authority in public positions or working for public agencies are prohibited from interfering with individuals who desire to exercise their religious beliefs in non-intrusive ways. It is often difficult for people to understand and follow those directives because they are often too selfish and egotistical to actually "do unto others as they would want others doing unto them." As Americans, we either have to treat others in that manner so that this becomes a land of freedom and opportunity for all people or close the door of freedom and opportunity on all who are not willing to become the kind of person that some think is the standard American. The war will not end or subside until that decision has been decisively made one way or the other. We cannot use the law and public policy to dictate social and moral ideas that reflect the position of one religious or ethnic group over others and expect America to become all that it can or should become. It would also show us up as being the ultimate hypocrites, based upon what we have declared throughout our history." If I hear one more time these folk on the Right stipulate that we want our country back, I will regurgitate. Who took their country? What America are they talking about the America depicted on those signs that show my President with a Hitler mustache, or my elegant and smart First Lady in a big Afro as my president walks into a function dressed like a pimp, or those Tea Party radicals or racist, you figure it out that called the Civil Rights icon John Lewis a nigger and spit on another representative as they walked by, that America I ask you. They can have that America but if it comes to fruition we will in fact be the biggest hypocrites as we go about the world espousing the attributes of democracy. This final article which was a reprint from a February 13-19 article by Charles Tisdale (I have quoted from the Jackson Advocate a lot because blacks in Mississippi relate to issues differently than the Michigan Chronicle also a black newspaper, I receive them both) Mr. Tisdale stated in an article entitled "Key to Progress" The *European is to other races of mankind what man himself is to lower animals; he makes them subservient to his use, and when he cannot subdue, he destroys them*! Alex de Tocqueville, *Democracy in America* Alex de[6] Tocqueville's ominous prophecy rings as true today as it did when he first promulgated this macabre theorem in 1735. The masses of African Americans are no longer necessary to this nation's military industrial complex. In fact, African Americans are now perceived as impediments to progress and are therefore expendable. African Americans, once the fodder which fueled this country's industrial machinery and provided the warm bodies for its wars, are now considered surplus, needed by neither this country's war machine nor its depleted industrial sector. Thus the solution to the problem of disposing of this country's excess and un-optimum African American population looms imminently for this country's economic establishment. The proposals postulated by military industrial complex to complete the "final solution" to the problem of America's unskilled African Americans are complex and sophisticated. However, without

[6] Article by Charles Tisdale, reprinted from the February 13-19 edition entitled "Key to Progress."

debate, and perhaps without complete authority, these plans made in the 1960s after Black insurrections swept through this nation's cities, have been completely implemented, according to a knowledgeable former intelligence official. To those who believe that AIDS, unchecked venereal diseases of other kinds, drugs and rumors of drug usage and sales in African American communities, the unfunding of community health resources and most of all, the failure to educate African American children are not all part and parcel of the agenda to not only "subdue" but "destroy" the African American people, I ask that they look at what's occurring in this city and state. The African Americans reign supreme over those the sell-outs pretend to speak for. As a whole, African Americans here are unable to protect their families from racist assaults whether launched by racist police officer like Steve Wilson, who killed anti-drug activist Johnnie Griffin or by public officials who fail to treat African Americans courteously. The principle beneficiaries of the political empowerment generated by the life blood of Fannie Lou Hamer, Martin Luther King, Medgar Evers, and Schwerner, Goodman and Chaney are the enemies of African Americans. African American people must come together or face annihilation by the very officials we thrust into office on the strength of our past insurgencies!"

I close with this thought that I read from an anonymous writer, "**If Pro is the opposite of Con, is Congress the opposite of Progress**?"

41250915R00062

Made in the USA
Charleston, SC
23 April 2015